EMMANUEL JOSEPH

From Arenas to AI, How Mythology and Technology Are Transforming Sports

First edition

This book was professionally typeset on Reedsy.
Find out more at reedsy.com

Contents

1

Chapter 1: The Dawn of Athletic Mythology

In the ancient world, sports were more than mere physical contests; they were sacred rituals that connected humanity to the divine. In Greece, the Olympic Games were held in honor of Zeus, the king of the gods, and athletes competed not just for personal glory, but for the favor of the divine. These events were steeped in mythology, with legends like Hercules inspiring feats of strength and endurance. The blend of athleticism and mythology instilled a sense of reverence and awe, making sports a central part of cultural identity.

As the centuries passed, different civilizations created their own mythologies surrounding sports. The Aztecs had their own ball game, tlachtli, which was not only a sport but also a religious ceremony with sacrificial undertones. These early forms of sports were a way for humans to connect with the cosmos, express their devotion, and celebrate human potential. The stories and legends that grew from these events became an integral part of the cultural fabric.

The role of sports in mythology wasn't limited to entertainment; it also served as a moral compass. Heroes like Achilles and Theseus demonstrated virtues such as bravery, honor, and perseverance. Their stories were told and retold, shaping societal values and inspiring individuals to strive for greatness. In many ways, the ancient world laid the groundwork for the enduring connection between sports and storytelling.

In conclusion, the dawn of athletic mythology set the stage for sports to become a powerful force in human culture. It was a time when physical prowess was intertwined with spiritual significance, and the legends that emerged continue to influence how we perceive sports today.

2

Chapter 2: The Evolution of Sports Arenas

The evolution of sports arenas mirrors the growth and transformation of human societies. In ancient Greece, the stadiums were simple open-air structures, where spectators gathered to watch athletes compete in the nude, a tradition that symbolized purity and the celebration of the human form. These early arenas were often located near temples, emphasizing the sacred nature of athletic competition.

As the Roman Empire rose to prominence, so did the grandeur of its sports arenas. The Colosseum, an architectural marvel, became a symbol of Roman engineering prowess and the brutal spectacle of gladiatorial combat. It was in these massive arenas that the populace found an escape from their daily lives, cheering for their favorite gladiators and witnessing awe-inspiring feats of bravery and skill. The Roman arenas were more than just venues for sport; they were a tool for political control, a way for emperors to gain favor with the masses.

With the fall of the Roman Empire, the grand arenas of the past fell into disrepair, and sports competitions took on a more localized and less organized form. Medieval jousting tournaments and village fairs became the new arenas where knights and commoners alike could showcase their skills. The evolution of sports arenas reflects the shifting priorities and resources of societies over time.

Today, modern sports arenas are technological marvels, equipped with advanced facilities that enhance both the athlete and spectator experience. From retractable roofs to giant LED screens, these arenas are designed to accommodate massive crowds and provide a seamless viewing experience. The evolution of sports arenas highlights the progression from sacred rituals to spectacles of entertainment and technological innovation.

3

Chapter 3: The Intersection of Myth and Modern Sports

In contemporary sports, the influence of mythology is still evident, although it has evolved to suit modern sensibilities. Athletes are often elevated to the status of modern-day heroes, their achievements celebrated and their stories mythologized. Icons like Michael Jordan, Serena Williams, and Usain Bolt have become cultural legends, their journeys inspiring millions around the globe.

The media plays a crucial role in shaping these modern myths. Through storytelling, documentaries, and coverage, the narratives of athletes are constructed, emphasizing their struggles, triumphs, and human qualities. This mythologization helps create a deeper connection between the athletes and their audience, fostering a sense of loyalty and admiration.

Moreover, the rituals and traditions associated with sports events echo the ancient ceremonies. The Olympic Games, with their elaborate opening ceremonies and torch relays, are a direct continuation of the ancient Greek traditions. Similarly, the Super Bowl halftime show has become a cultural phenomenon, blending entertainment with ritualistic elements that captivate audiences worldwide.

In essence, the intersection of myth and modern sports reveals that the core human desire for storytelling and hero-worship remains unchanged. While the context and medium have evolved, the fundamental connection between mythology and sports continues to shape how we perceive and engage with athletic events.

4

Chapter 4: The Rise of Sports Technology

The rise of technology has revolutionized the world of sports, transforming how athletes train, compete, and recover. Advances in sports science have led to the development of cutting-edge equipment, data analytics, and performance-enhancing techniques that push the boundaries of human potential. Wearable technology, such as fitness trackers and smart clothing, allows athletes to monitor their vitals in real-time, optimizing their performance and minimizing the risk of injury.

Data analytics has become a game-changer, providing coaches and athletes with valuable insights into their performance. By analyzing metrics such as speed, distance, and heart rate, teams can devise strategies and training programs tailored to individual athletes' needs. This data-driven approach has led to remarkable improvements in performance, as athletes can now train with unprecedented precision and efficiency.

Virtual reality (VR) and augmented reality (AR) have also made their mark in sports, offering immersive training experiences that were once unimaginable. VR simulations allow athletes to practice in a controlled environment, refining their skills and visualizing game scenarios. AR, on the other hand, enhances the viewing experience for fans, providing real-time statistics and interactive elements that bring them closer to the action.

As technology continues to advance, its impact on sports will only grow. From injury prevention to fan engagement, the rise of sports technology is

7

reshaping the landscape of athletic competition, making it more dynamic, accessible, and exciting for everyone involved.

5

Chapter 5: The Digital Transformation of Fan Engagement

The digital age has ushered in a new era of fan engagement, transforming how audiences interact with their favorite sports and athletes. Social media platforms like Twitter, Instagram, and TikTok have become essential tools for athletes to connect with their fans, share their journey, and build their personal brand. This direct line of communication has humanized athletes, allowing fans to see beyond the game and gain insight into their lives.

Live streaming and on-demand content have revolutionized the way fans consume sports. No longer confined to traditional broadcast schedules, fans can now watch games and highlights whenever and wherever they want. This accessibility has expanded the reach of sports, bringing in new audiences from around the globe and fostering a more inclusive and diverse fan base.

Esports has emerged as a significant player in the world of sports, attracting millions of fans and generating substantial revenue. Competitive gaming tournaments, streamed live on platforms like Twitch and YouTube, have captivated audiences and created new opportunities for fan engagement. The rise of esports demonstrates the evolving nature of sports entertainment and the growing influence of digital technology.

In this digital era, fan engagement is more interactive and immersive than ever before. Virtual fan experiences, such as attending games in VR or participating in augmented reality scavenger hunts, offer unique and memorable interactions. The digital transformation of fan engagement has created a more connected and engaged sports community, bridging the gap between athletes and their supporters.

6

Chapter 6: The Ethics of Technology in Sports

As technology continues to permeate the world of sports, ethical considerations have come to the forefront. The use of performance-enhancing technology, such as prosthetics and genetic modification, raises questions about fairness and the integrity of competition. While these advancements can offer incredible benefits, they also blur the line between natural talent and artificial enhancement.

The issue of data privacy is another ethical concern. With the rise of wearable technology and data analytics, vast amounts of personal information are collected from athletes. Ensuring that this data is handled responsibly and securely is crucial to protecting athletes' privacy and maintaining trust. Striking the right balance between technological innovation and ethical responsibility is essential for the future of sports.

Furthermore, the impact of technology on the spirit of sportsmanship is a topic of debate. While instant replay and video assistant referee (VAR) systems have improved the accuracy of officiating, they also disrupt the flow of the game and can lead to contentious decisions. Finding a way to integrate technology without compromising the essence of sportsmanship is a challenge that the industry must address.

In conclusion, the ethical considerations surrounding technology in sports are complex and multifaceted. As we continue to push the boundaries of what is possible, it is essential to navigate these challenges thoughtfully and responsibly, ensuring that the integrity and spirit of sports are preserved.

7

Chapter 7: The Future of Sports Arenas

As we look to the future, sports arenas are set to undergo a transformation driven by technological advancements and changing fan expectations. The stadiums of tomorrow will be smart, sustainable, and immersive, offering unparalleled experiences for both athletes and spectators. Innovations such as 5G connectivity, artificial intelligence, and eco-friendly design will redefine what it means to attend a live sports event.

Smart stadiums will be equipped with sensors and IoT devices that monitor and optimize various aspects of the venue, from crowd management to energy consumption. These intelligent systems will enhance the overall experience, ensuring that fans can enjoy the event seamlessly and comfortably. Real-time data analytics will provide valuable insights, enabling stadium operators to make informed decisions and improve their services.

Sustainability will be a key focus in the design of future sports arenas. Eco-friendly materials, energy-efficient systems, and waste reduction strategies will minimize the environmental impact of these massive structures. By prioritizing sustainability, sports organizations can lead the way in promoting environmental stewardship and inspiring positive change.

Immersive technologies, such as augmented reality and holographic displays, will elevate the fan experience to new heights. Imagine watching a game where real-time stats and player information are projected onto the field, or where holographic replays allow you to relive key moments from multiple angles. These innovations will create a more interactive and engaging atmosphere, making every game a memorable event.

Additionally, future sports arenas will prioritize accessibility and inclusivity. Advanced facilities and technologies will ensure that everyone, regardless of physical ability, can enjoy the full experience of attending a live event. From barrier-free seating to augmented reality guides, these stadiums will set a new standard for inclusivity, making sports more welcoming and enjoyable for all fans.

The integration of smart technology, sustainability, and immersive experiences will redefine the concept of sports arenas. These futuristic venues will not only serve as sites for athletic competition but also as hubs of technological innovation and cultural significance.

8

Chapter 8: The Role of Artificial Intelligence in Sports

Artificial intelligence (AI) has begun to play a transformative role in the world of sports, offering unprecedented capabilities in areas such as performance analysis, strategy development, and fan engagement. AI-powered tools can analyze vast amounts of data to identify patterns and trends that would be impossible for humans to detect. This enables coaches and athletes to make more informed decisions, optimize training programs, and develop winning strategies.

One of the most significant applications of AI in sports is in injury prevention and rehabilitation. AI algorithms can analyze an athlete's biomechanics and detect early signs of potential injuries, allowing for timely intervention and reducing the risk of long-term damage. Additionally, AI-driven rehabilitation programs can be tailored to the specific needs of each athlete, ensuring a more effective and efficient recovery process.

AI is also revolutionizing the fan experience by providing personalized content and recommendations. From tailored highlights and statistics to interactive chatbots and virtual assistants, AI enhances how fans engage with their favorite sports and teams. This level of personalization creates a more immersive and satisfying experience, deepening the connection between fans and the sports they love.

As AI continues to evolve, its impact on sports will only grow, offering new opportunities for innovation and improvement. The integration of AI in sports demonstrates the potential of technology to enhance every aspect of athletic competition, from performance and strategy to fan engagement and safety.

9

Chapter 9: The Globalization of Sports

The globalization of sports has connected athletes and fans from all corners of the world, creating a diverse and dynamic landscape. International competitions such as the FIFA World Cup, the Olympics, and the NBA have brought together the best athletes from different countries, showcasing their talents on a global stage. These events foster a sense of unity and camaraderie, transcending cultural and geographic boundaries.

The rise of digital technology has played a crucial role in the globalization of sports. Social media platforms, live streaming services, and international broadcasting networks have made it easier for fans to follow their favorite sports and athletes, regardless of their location. This increased accessibility has expanded the reach of sports, bringing in new audiences and fostering a more inclusive global community.

The globalization of sports has also led to the cross-pollination of ideas and techniques, as athletes and coaches learn from their international counterparts. This exchange of knowledge and expertise has elevated the level of competition and innovation, driving the evolution of sports to new heights.

In conclusion, the globalization of sports has created a more interconnected and diverse world of athletic competition. As technology continues to break down barriers, the global sports community will only grow stronger, fostering a sense of unity and shared passion for the love of the game.

18

10

Chapter 10: The Impact of Technology on Training and Performance

The integration of technology in sports training has revolutionized how athletes prepare for competition. From advanced biomechanical analysis to personalized training programs, technology has enabled athletes to optimize their performance and reach new levels of excellence. Wearable devices, such as smartwatches and fitness trackers, provide real-time data on an athlete's vitals, allowing for precise monitoring and adjustment of training routines.

Biomechanical analysis tools, such as motion capture systems and force plates, offer detailed insights into an athlete's movement patterns and physical performance. This information helps coaches identify areas for improvement and develop targeted training programs that enhance strength, speed, and agility. The use of technology in training has led to more efficient and effective workouts, reducing the risk of injury and maximizing performance gains.

Virtual reality and augmented reality have also made their mark in sports training, offering immersive environments for athletes to practice and refine their skills. VR simulations allow athletes to experience game scenarios in a controlled setting, while AR provides real-time feedback and guidance during training sessions. These technologies create a more engaging and effective training experience, helping athletes prepare for the challenges of competition.

The impact of technology on training and performance is profound, offering new opportunities for innovation and improvement. As technology continues to advance, athletes and coaches will have even more tools at their disposal to achieve peak performance and push the boundaries of what is possible.

11

Chapter 11: The Future of Sports Medicine

The field of sports medicine has benefited greatly from technological advancements, leading to improved injury prevention, diagnosis, and treatment. Innovations such as regenerative medicine, minimally invasive surgery, and advanced imaging techniques have transformed the way injuries are managed and treated. These developments have not only enhanced the recovery process but also extended the careers of many athletes.

Regenerative medicine, including stem cell therapy and platelet-rich plasma (PRP) treatments, has shown promise in promoting the healing of damaged tissues and reducing recovery times. These cutting-edge therapies harness the body's natural healing processes, offering new hope for athletes with chronic injuries or degenerative conditions. As research in this field progresses, regenerative medicine is expected to play an increasingly important role in sports medicine.

Minimally invasive surgical techniques, such as arthroscopy, have revolutionized the treatment of sports injuries. These procedures involve smaller incisions, resulting in less tissue damage and faster recovery times. Advanced imaging techniques, such as MRI and ultrasound, allow for more accurate diagnosis and assessment of injuries, enabling targeted and effective treatment plans.

In addition to these advancements, the integration of AI and data analytics in sports medicine has improved injury prevention and rehabilitation. AI algorithms can analyze an athlete's biomechanics and detect early signs of potential injuries, allowing for timely intervention and reducing the risk of long-term damage. Data-driven rehabilitation programs can be tailored to the specific needs of each athlete, ensuring a more effective and efficient recovery process.

The future of sports medicine is bright, with ongoing research and technological innovations poised to further enhance the field. As new treatments and techniques are developed, athletes will benefit from improved care and support, enabling them to perform at their best and enjoy longer, healthier careers.

12

Chapter 12: The Convergence of Mythology and Technology in Sports

As we look to the future, the convergence of mythology and technology in sports will continue to shape how we perceive and engage with athletic competition. Modern athletes will be celebrated as heroes, their stories mythologized and shared through digital platforms. Technology will play a central role in enhancing the fan experience, making sports more accessible, interactive, and immersive.

The storytelling aspect of sports will evolve, with AI and digital media creating new ways to share and preserve the legends of athletes. Virtual reality and augmented reality will allow fans to experience the history and mythology of sports in immersive and interactive ways, deepening their connection to the athletes and the events they love.

As technology continues to advance, it will also transform the way athletes train, compete, and recover. The integration of AI, data analytics, and advanced medical treatments will push the boundaries of human potential, enabling athletes to achieve feats once thought impossible. The future of sports will be a dynamic and exciting blend of tradition and innovation, where the legends of the past inspire the breakthroughs of tomorrow.

13

Chapter 13: The Influence of Sports on Popular Culture

Sports have always had a significant impact on popular culture, shaping trends, fashion, and entertainment. Athletes often become cultural icons, influencing everything from clothing styles to music and film. The crossover between sports and popular culture creates a unique synergy that captures the imagination of fans worldwide.

The fashion industry has long been inspired by sports, with athletic wear becoming a staple in everyday fashion. Brands like Nike, Adidas, and Under Armour have capitalized on this trend, creating clothing lines that blend performance and style. Athletes themselves often collaborate with designers to launch their own fashion lines, further blurring the lines between sports and fashion.

In the entertainment industry, sports have provided rich material for movies, television shows, and music. Films like "Rocky," "Remember the Titans," and "Space Jam" have become cultural touchstones, celebrating the triumphs and struggles of athletes. Music, too, has been influenced by sports, with artists penning songs that capture the spirit of competition and victory.

The influence of sports on popular culture extends beyond fashion and entertainment. Sports stars often use their platform to advocate for social and political causes, raising awareness and inspiring change. This intersection of sports and activism highlights the powerful role that athletes play in shaping societal values and driving progress.

25

14

Chapter 14: The Role of Sports in Education and Youth Development

Sports play a crucial role in education and youth development, offering numerous benefits that extend beyond physical fitness. Participation in sports teaches valuable life skills, such as teamwork, discipline, and resilience, that are essential for personal growth and success. Schools and communities recognize the importance of sports in fostering well-rounded individuals and providing opportunities for youth to thrive.

Physical education programs in schools emphasize the importance of regular exercise and the development of motor skills. These programs also promote healthy competition, encouraging students to set goals, work hard, and strive for improvement. Through sports, students learn the value of perseverance and the satisfaction that comes from achieving their goals.

Extracurricular sports programs offer additional opportunities for youth to engage in physical activity and develop social skills. Team sports, in particular, foster a sense of camaraderie and belonging, helping young people build friendships and develop a strong sense of community. Coaches and mentors play a vital role in guiding and supporting young athletes, helping them navigate the challenges of adolescence and build self-confidence.

Furthermore, sports can provide a pathway to higher education and future careers. Scholarships and athletic programs at colleges and universities offer opportunities for talented athletes to pursue their academic and athletic aspirations. The lessons learned through sports—such as leadership, time management, and goal-setting—equip young people with the skills they need to succeed in all areas of life.

15

Chapter 15: The Intersection of Sports and Mental Health

The connection between sports and mental health has garnered increasing attention in recent years, as athletes and experts recognize the impact of physical activity on psychological well-being. Participation in sports can promote mental health by reducing stress, improving mood, and enhancing overall quality of life. However, the pressures of competition and performance can also present mental health challenges that must be addressed.

Regular physical activity has been shown to release endorphins, which are natural mood lifters. Engaging in sports provides an outlet for stress and anxiety, offering a healthy way to cope with life's challenges. The sense of accomplishment and self-efficacy that comes from achieving athletic goals can boost self-esteem and confidence, contributing to a positive self-image.

At the same time, the competitive nature of sports can create mental health challenges for athletes. The pressure to perform, fear of failure, and expectations from coaches, fans, and sponsors can lead to anxiety, depression, and burnout. It is essential for athletes to have access to mental health resources and support systems to navigate these challenges and maintain their well-being.

The conversation around mental health in sports has gained momentum, with high-profile athletes speaking out about their experiences and advocating for change. By addressing the mental health needs of athletes, the sports community can create a more supportive and inclusive environment that prioritizes the well-being of its members.

Chapter 16: The Economic Impact of Sports

The economic impact of sports is significant, contributing to local and global economies through various channels. Sports events, teams, and related industries generate substantial revenue, create jobs, and stimulate economic growth. The financial influence of sports extends beyond ticket sales and merchandise, encompassing tourism, media rights, and infrastructure development.

Major sporting events, such as the Olympics, the FIFA World Cup, and the Super Bowl, attract millions of spectators and generate billions of dollars in revenue. These events boost local economies by attracting tourists, filling hotels, and increasing spending at restaurants, shops, and entertainment venues. The economic benefits of hosting such events can have a lasting impact, as improved infrastructure and increased visibility can attract future investment and tourism.

Sports teams and leagues also contribute to economic growth by creating jobs and supporting related industries. From stadium employees and team staff to media professionals and merchandise vendors, the sports industry provides diverse employment opportunities. Additionally, the construction and maintenance of sports facilities stimulate the economy through investment and job creation.

The media rights and broadcasting deals associated with sports generate substantial revenue for leagues, teams, and networks. The global reach of sports content has led to lucrative partnerships and sponsorships, further fueling economic growth. The economic impact of sports is a testament to its significance as a driving force in the global economy.

17

Chapter 17: The Future of Sports: Innovation and Transformation

As we look to the future, the world of sports is poised for continued innovation and transformation. Advances in technology, changes in societal values, and evolving fan expectations will shape the future of athletic competition, creating new opportunities and challenges. The future of sports will be characterized by a dynamic blend of tradition and innovation, pushing the boundaries of what is possible.

Technology will continue to play a central role in the evolution of sports, enhancing performance, training, and fan engagement. Innovations such as AI, VR, AR, and wearable devices will redefine how athletes train, compete, and recover, pushing the limits of human potential. The integration of smart technology in sports arenas and facilities will create more immersive and interactive experiences for fans, setting new standards for live events.

Societal values and cultural shifts will also influence the future of sports. The emphasis on inclusivity, diversity, and sustainability will drive changes in how sports are organized and perceived. Efforts to promote gender equality, environmental stewardship, and social responsibility will shape the policies and practices of sports organizations, creating a more equitable and sustainable future.

The future of sports will also be shaped by the changing expectations of fans. As digital natives become the dominant demographic, the demand for interactive, personalized, and on-demand content will continue to grow. Sports organizations will need to adapt to these preferences, offering engaging and accessible experiences that cater to a diverse and global audience.

In conclusion, the future of sports is a dynamic and exciting landscape, characterized by innovation, transformation, and the enduring power of athletic competition. As we navigate this ever-changing world, the convergence of mythology and technology will continue to shape how we perceive and engage with sports, inspiring new legends and pushing the boundaries of human achievement.

From Arenas to AI: How Mythology and Technology Are Transforming Sports

This enlightening book explores the remarkable journey of sports from ancient arenas to the high-tech world of artificial intelligence. **"From Arenas to AI: How Mythology and Technology Are Transforming Sports"** delves into the rich history and cultural significance of sports, highlighting how mythology once infused athletic competitions with divine meaning. It examines the evolution of sports arenas, tracing their development from simple structures to modern, technologically advanced stadiums that offer immersive experiences for fans.

The book also investigates the impact of technology on sports, from performance-enhancing equipment and data analytics to virtual reality training and AI-driven fan engagement. It addresses the ethical considerations that come with these advancements and explores the future of sports medicine, injury prevention, and rehabilitation.

In addition, the book sheds light on the globalization of sports, the influence of sports on popular culture, and the role of sports in education and youth development. It highlights the importance of mental health in the athletic community and the economic impact of sports on local and global economies.

Through captivating storytelling and insightful analysis, this book offers a comprehensive look at the dynamic intersection of mythology and technology in sports. It celebrates the enduring spirit of athletic competition and the limitless possibilities that lie ahead, making it a must-read for sports enthusiasts, athletes, and anyone fascinated by the ever-evolving world of sports.